DETOX YOUR SPIRIT

40 DAY PERSONAL DEVOTION TO CHANGE YOUR LIFE

(devotions, prayers & declarations)

By

Apostle Charles Magaiza

Detox Your Spirit is a 40 day devotional directly inspired by the Holy Spirit to transform your life. Throughout scripture the number of days is significant, we see lives changed in 40 days.

This book is from the bestselling author of **21 Days of Fasting & Prayer**. It will help you reactivate and reenergize your spirit. Through the devotions, prayers and declarations, you will overcome every spiritual huddle and receive healing, deliverance and breakthrough in every area of need. You will come to an awareness of your rights in Christ.

INDEX

Section 1: My prayer for you

Section 2: Don't be doubtful, believe

Section 3: Turn on the power

Section 4: Power of words

Section 5: Grow in knowledge

Section 6- Bill of rights

INTRODUCTION

Since ancient times, human beings have known that the accumulation of certain toxins in the body is a significant cause of disease, aging and death. The solution has always been to *detox* the body. There are moments when I have felt a spiritual clutter in my life and to break this, the Holy Spirit has always prompted me to go on a 40 day fast and prayer season to de clutter- more like a spiritual *detox*. This has always come with tremendous results. Year in and year out, I have found myself having to engage in this 40 day journey. It has always been a time to find the heart of God and turn away from my own selfish direction and re-establish where God's heart is for my life. I know that you are here because you have a deeper yearning for God.

Why 40 days? In the Bible, we see many lives that God transformed in 40 days. Noah's life was transformed by 40 days and 40 nights of rain, the Egyptian embalming took 40 days, Moses was in the mountain and fasted for 40 days and 40 nights and there he received instructions from God. When he came down, his face was radiant with the glory of the Lord. The 12 spies that went into the Promised Land searched out the land for 40 days. Nineveh was given 40 days to repent during the time of Jonah the prophet. Jesus fasted for 40 days and 40 nights when He was driven into the wilderness by the Holy Spirit. During this time angels ministered to Him. The next 40 days are going to be your time to receive the ministry of angels! When Jesus rose from the dead, He hung around for 40 days.

The next 40 days are going to be life transforming for you. You will be a force to reckon. As I have engaged in this 40 days journey, God has spoken different things to me. Some of the devotions I share here are directly from my prayer journal where I note the direct words of God to me. I have no doubt that these words will be a blessing to your soul in the next 40 days.

Get ready for a life transforming journey as you turn your life around for good.

SECTION 1
I PRAY FOR YOU

We begin this journey with 2 special prayers. It is important that I pray for you so that your journey will be Spirit filled and fulfilling.

DAY 1

*For this cause I bow my knees unto
the Father of our Lord Jesus Christ,*

*Of whom the whole family in heaven
and earth is named,*

(Eph 3:14-15 KJV)

I pray for you, as a member of the family of
God here on earth. As one who is washed and
sanctified by the blood of Jesus Christ!

May order come into your estate and all things
that were disorderly in your life meet with order! I pray that the Spirit of the Lord would take
full charge of your affairs and cause you to
move from that place of limitation to a place
of victory and power. May you see increase in
your days and may the power of toil be broken today.

Every satanic force that was working against
you is losing its grip today. I command every
evil spirit to let go of your business, children,

11

husband or wife, job, friends and all that's yours. I command every evil spirit to let go of your health in the name of Jesus. As the Word declares, by the stripes of Jesus on the cross you were healed, you will be a witness of this word in your life today. Healing is your portion today in Jesus' name!

I pray for ideas. Life changing ideas! Ideas that will take you to another level in your life! As the anointing of God operates in you, I pray that you receive the grace to implement things. As you cast your nets into the deep, may your catch be net breaking and boat sinking. I pray that the blessing be visible on you so that the whole world will know that you are a child of God.

I pray for long life over you. I remove every demonic force that brings sudden terror and tragedy. May you live until you are satisfied! I pray that the Spirit of God will direct you and keep you away from harm. I pray that angels walk with you and be your rear guard.

I pray for your finances. May God's grace overshadow your resources! May you not lack and may all your needs be met! I pray that you will have in excess for every charitable donation. May you receive properties in this season! I speak the wisdom of God that will give you grace to have reserves that can impact generations ahead.

- **Declaration**

- I declare today, you are trouble proof, fear proof, poverty proof and death proof. You are repelling every satanic force and every work that the devil is up to in this season. I declare a covering of God's Spirit over you, to equip you for a season such as this. I pronounce you victorious. I pronounce you fruitful. I pronounce you blessed. Say I AGREE!

DAY 2

That he would grant you, according to the riches of his glory, to be strengthened with might by his Spirit in the inner man;

That Christ may dwell in your hearts by faith; that ye, being rooted and grounded in love,

(Eph 3:16-17)

I pray for you as a special child of a loving God. May every storm that has been raging in your life be abated today! May you experience calmness in every area of your life! May calmness come into your marriage, business, finances and health!

May Jehovah grant you according to the riches of his glory, strength in the inner man by His Spirit! The riches of his glory are never run down; they are never depleted and never valueless. As this touches you, may intelligence be your portion, wisdom to confound the world.

May knowledge become a part of your life as a member of the family of God here on earth!

May you become conscious of the indwelling Christ! He lives in you; He is in every fibre of your being. He is in your bones, hair, muscles, gluttons, nerves and blood. I banish everything that is trying to invade these areas. May Christ sit as king in you, not pain, not cancer, not diabetes or any other evil disease known to man and not known to man!

I command victories without number in your life. As Christ is crowned king in your life, the world will know whose you are. I pray that every place you were mocked be eradicated today. Every place were voices have been raised to mock you and to pull you down be exterminated today as you walk strengthened by His Spirit in the inner man.

As the word says, He will give His angels charge over you. May angels come into battle on your behalf! I pray for the release of warring angels to fight for you, prosperity angels to gather wealth for you, angels of peace to enforce order in all the storms in your life.

I pray that you be granted **VIP** access into secret treasures. May your prayers overcome huddles and may answers to your requests be quick and immediate. I put lines of demarcation against the devil in your life. No demon will come near your house. There is no weapon, no magic charm and no sorcery that is manufactured against you that will prosper. May your fear factor be replaced with a faith factor as you overcome every obstacle in Jesus' name!

- **Declaration**

- I declare, you will not die but live to proclaim the might works of God. Your life will be a testimony for the world to witness the glory of the Lord.

detox

SECTION 2
DON'T BE DOUBFUL, BELIEVE!

Everything begins with faith, you must build your faith strong. In the following 12 days, we will focus on strengthening your faith. Remember, without faith it is impossible to please God.

DAY 3

In solemn truth I tell you that if any one shall say to this mountain, 'Remove, and hurl thyself into the sea,' and has no doubt about it in his heart, but steadfastly believes that what he says will happen, it shall be granted him.

(Mark 11:23 WNT)

Faith speaks in confidence. It is a child of a heart which is full of conviction of the truth of the Word of God. It is not sense knowledge devotion which awaits the confirmation that comes from the senses. Faith is not swayed by the surroundings and noisy circumstances.

The fig tree received one word from Jesus, to the natural eye, it didn't wither at that same time but Jesus did not stress Himself about it. He proceeded with his trip. The following morning, Peter saw that the Words spoken yesterday had had an effect on the tree. It was withered from the roots. The answer from Jesus was that

18

of total confidence, He took the opportunity to teach his pupils, *"If any one shall say to this mountain."* There is no one excluded from exploits that are through faith; anyone qualifies to operate in this result bringing faith.

The speaking of the one who is full of faith is that of persuasion. There is no vacillation or doubt on the words spoken. The heart is steadfast, not swayed by the outside appearance of things. This kind of faith brings things, it is not denied! It collects things that are not visible to the optical eye. This is the God kind of faith.

There are many things that are available for this kind of faith. It is progressive and pregnant with supernatural results. Many have failed to reap the rewards that faith brings because of their focus on the senses and the desire to seek assurance from them. Faith will make one appear absurd to the world of senses. It might even bring scorn only to be acknowledged by many when they have seen the results in it.

You can believe without wavering that in this year, things will turn around for your own good. You can trust and be confident that through faith, that disease has no residence in you. You can believe for a change in your finances as faith was before money. When God created the universe He used faith. He spoke things into existence. Faith is the new currency- it is the new money. Use it to move forward!

- **Declaration**

- Mountains are moving today, hurling themselves into the sea because of my faith. Mountains of sickness are moving, debt Mountains, Poverty Mountains and all sorts of mountains! I speak without fear and doubt, I declare and I will see it come to pass.

Day 4

"There's a little boy here who has five barley loaves and two fish. But that's a drop in the bucket for a crowd like this."

(John 6:9 MSG)

It was a massive crowd, three days without food in a wilderness. They didn't have anything to replenish their bodies with but still they wanted to hear more of the life giving words Jesus spoke. Lack of food was going to be the party spoiler but through faith, it was not a hopeless situation.

Jesus asks Philip, where shall we buy bread for all these people? He was scrutinizing him to see what he would say for Jesus already knew what he would do. Philip looked at the condition of the coffers and answered that two hundred pennyworth of bread was not enough. Andrew spoke; there is a little boy with five barley loaves and two fish- a drop in the bucket for a huge crowd. For Jesus, it was a perfect situation for the demonstration of Heavy Duty Faith.

Jesus was going to unleash faith to turn things around for good! He asked the people to sit down in anticipation of food. He was seeing the food multiplied without a shadow of doubt in Him. It is like setting the dinner table for the visitors when there is no food in the house and asking the visitors to wash their hands and wait for food. The result was an amazing testimony in the kingdom of God and a devastating sword in the domain of the enemy. A hungry multitude in the wilderness was fed with twelve baskets of excess collected.

Let me speak to you today, your faith can turn any wilderness situation into a joyous celebration. Like Philip, don't look at what you have as a means to the supply. Like Andrew, don't question the ability of little turning into much. Turn your faith on for overwhelming results. Philip looked at the things as they appeared and doubted. Don't look at the doctor's report, don't look at your wallet, and don't look at the world system- discharge your heavy duty faith on stubborn circumstances for heavy duty results! Circumstances must not dominate you- you must dominate circumstances.

- **Declaration**

- I declare there is provision available in my life right now needing to be triggered by my faith. I shock the devil by changing the field where this game of life is played through faith. Faith gives me an inequitable advantage over the world- this is the victory that overcomes the world even my faith.

Day 5

Under utterly hopeless circumstances he hopefully believed, so that he might become the forefather of many nations, in agreement with the words "EQUALLY NUMEROUS SHALL YOUR POSTERITY BE."

(Rom 4:18 WNT)

Circumstances are the state of affairs; it is the way things are looking right now to the natural eye. The one who will make progress is the one who will dominate circumstances. Abraham's state of affairs was hopeless. In the eyes of man, there was no way a child would come out of that situation. Now in hopelessness, Abraham hopefully believed. His believing was targeted at bringing results in the situation; he would become the forefather of many nations.

Abraham had the option of contemplating his vital powers which were now decayed. He had the option of contemplating Sarah's womb which was now in the mortuary. This he

24

did not do, he looked at the Word spoken, at the promise given and unleashed his faith on stubborn circumstances. He kept his eye on the Word, never wavering and never looking at anything else.

I am talking to you; yes you who wanted a child and you received all sorts of reports from the doctors. Your situation is no worse than what Abraham had to overcome. Don't walk by sight, walk by faith. Begin to see that baby boy, yes the one with the dimples. See that baby girl; yes the one with the curly hair. The eyes of faith will always collect what they see. Don't ever allow your natural sight to be stronger than your faith. I am talking to you who have been bankrupted by a business deal gone wrong. I am talking to you who are in need of a job. Whatever the situation, your faith can triumph over it.

Faith will unlock rivers in dry places; it will bring harvests in parched lands. Faith will change the destiny of families and nations. It is a defence against circumstances that are meant to discourage you. It is a shield that beats the fiery darts of the enemy hands down. You will advance in this season; you will see the hand of God over you as you start walking and speaking in faith. Your life will be a testimony;

the celebrations are in your house this time around. You will tell others of the goodness of God. Shout THAT IS ME!

- **Declaration**

- My faith unlocks great value today. I stand on the word of God and refuse to look at the circumstances around me. Like Abraham I believe and I know every dream will come to life in Jesus' name.

Day 6

Then enquired he of them the hour when he began to amend. And they said unto him, Yesterday at the seventh hour the fever left him.

(John 4:52 KJV)

When Jesus came again to Cana of Galilee, there was a royal official whose son was lying ill in Capernaum. When he met Jesus, he began to beg Him to come down and cure his son who was at the point of death. Jesus was quick in rebuking him, "Unless you see signs and miracles you will not believe at all." The nobleman undeterred continued to plead for the life of his son.

There is something that Jesus was demanding from this man, he had to believe before seeing anything. Faith will acknowledge the truth of the Word of God where there is no sign to prove it. Faith doesn't flow in the same channel as the human senses. When Jesus saw the persistence in this man, He gave him a Word,

"Go in peace, your son will live!" (v50). There is a response that you must give to the release of a Word and this man was on point. He put his trust in what Jesus said and started going home. He entered a place of rest because of the Word that came from the Master of Life.

What is your own response to the Word? Do you rest on the promise knowing that you hold an answer already? When you have brought something in prayer to God, do you continue nagging Him for a sign to prove that the answer will come?

On his way home, the nobleman met his servants who told him that his son was off the death bed. He asked them, "At what hour did he begin to amend?" They told him and he knew it was the very hour when Jesus had given him the Word.

The point of believing is the point of receiving. The child began to amend when Jesus released the Word and the man believed *(unleashed his faith for definite results)*. There are things in your life today that will be amended by your believing. You don't have to see with your eyes first but enter your rest in the Word of God.

28

Your finances will begin to amend if you believe, your marriage will amend, sickness will
amend in obedience to the Word but you
must believe to see this. Blessed are those who
believe without seeing.

- **Declaration**

- I declare and decree that things are
  amending around you! You will not walk
  in fear anymore but in faith. I declare that
  your faith is collecting for you high defini-
  tion results.

Day 7

...men who, as the result of faith, conquered whole kingdoms, brought about true justice, obtained promises from God, stopped lions' mouths,

deprived fire of its power, escaped being killed by the sword, out of weakness were made strong, became mighty in war, put to flight foreign armies.

(Heb 11:33-34 WNT)

Faith is not like the currencies of the nations that change their value from time to time and from place to place. The worth of is inestimable in every nation. With it is the ability to unlock any situation. Faith has always been God's way- His method and technique which He has extended to us his children to operate in his very league.

30

Scripture tells us, "With God all things are possible *(Matt 19:26)*." As the light of this revelation becomes brighter in you, you will see it, "Only believe and all things are possible to him that believes *(Mark 9:23)*." Faith is a method of Deity and coming into the life of faith is transformational- it raises one to a level of operation as of the Father.

Hebrews shows us that some of the Old Testament folk plugged into this life of faith and they were never the same. They pulled off tremendous feats through faith but they never got the fulfilment of the great promise- the Messiah Christ Jesus.

From the history of faith, we perceive that it conquers whole kingdoms, it brings about true justice, it obtains promises from God, and it stops the mouths of lions. When Daniel was thrown into that den of lions, he was so full of faith it evoked a wall of protection around him. By faith, thrown in the fire, they deprived fire of its power. This fire that was heated seven times over but faith penetrated it and held the power of fire captive. This is strong! Faith dispossessed fire of its power. Faith gave escapes from death by the sword. Faith touched those that were weak and they made comebacks and becoming mighty in war they put foreign armies to flight. Every foreign army that was invading you is going on down today.

Faith is a multipurpose weapon, an instrument that is precise in its implementation. It snatches victory from the jaws of defeat. It turns a death bed into a starting point. It redefines what is known as reality. It operates in the order of deity with supernatural results all the time.

- **Declaration**

- Today, I operate this instrument called faith over my situation. I employ faith over my marriage and job; I evoke it over my business. I let faith be the precision instrument of the surgeon to remove that cancer. I let faith pin point the virus in my body and eliminate it. I let faith turn things around in my life and bring about unfathomable victories. Faith is placing me in a higher order of victory.

Day 8

Looking unto Jesus the author and finisher of our faith; who for the joy that was set before him endured the cross, despising the shame, and is set down at the right hand of the throne of God.

(Heb 12:2 KJV)

The position of your focus determines the progression of your story. Faith demands for one to focus on a constant object and the world we live in is never constant. Surrendering your focus on the world and its events means that you will never have a moment of rest.

The writer of Hebrews points us to Jesus, the chief leader, captain and the consummator of our faith. He faced the cross which had shame in it but He chose to ignore the gory details of the cross and chose rather to look at the joy that was after the cross. He chose to despise the shame associated with dying on the cross but rather focussed on the results of it all. Today, He is gloriously sitting at the right hand of the throne of God, a sign of victory over all the work of His enemies.

As you move forward in faith, there are times were taking a stand of faith might mean shame and pain. Well, the captain of our faith has shown us the example. Shift your eyes from the chaos and focus on Jesus. He is a constant; focusing on Him will assure you of joy in the midst of the chaos. Peace will accompany you in the midst of the storm.

You will produce results because of faith. Don't allow the challenges around you to snub you of the prize of your faith. There is rest ahead for those who endure in faith. Whatsoever is born of God is victorious over the world and faith is that victory that conquers the world *(1 John 5:4)*. Unleash your faith on stubborn circumstances as you keep your eyes on Jesus.

- **Declaration**

- My business is turning around because of faith, disease has lost its power over me and I shift my focus from it to the Captain and completer of my faith! My marriage is turning around for good. The elusive is be-

coming an easy find for me. Faith pleases
God and today it is positioning me in His
presence.

Day 9

Then saith he to Thomas, Reach hither thy finger, and behold my hands; and reach hither thy hand, and thrust it into my side: and be not faithless, but believing.

(Job 20:27 KJV)

Faith puts you in a season of unprecedented miracles signs and wonders. As you believe in an unusual manner, God will come through for you in unusual ways.

Thomas is known today as the doubting Thomas. This characteristic of doubt was apparent when the other disciples saw the risen Christ in his absence. When they related the encounter to him, he said he would not believe without seeing. After eight days, Jesus entered the room which was locked by the way but He showed up. I don't care what has locked you in, Jesus is showing up. There is no place in which He is denied access.

Thomas' faith was fragile and frail- it was sense knowledge faith. It needed to see, to feel, to reach out in the physical for it to find satisfaction. Jesus rebuked him, "be not faithless but believing." Despise the Thomas kind of faith and reach out for the pure faith that believes on the Word. Faith that anchors fully on what the Word has said and doesn't wait for the satisfaction of the senses!

I launch you into the month of March loaded with the ability to bring transformation and change. I position you for exploits and I know that the Lord who has begun a great work in you will finish it in this season.

Ephesians 3:20 tells us that our God is loaded with the ability to exceed our wildest imaginations in prayer according to the power that is at work inside us. Hallelujah that power is inside you! You must carry it this month into your job, business, family, university and school.

- **Declaration**

- I speak into your life right now, that El Shaddai God will load your life with miracle surprises in this season. Those that were gathering against you are gathering to scatter. Every plan against you is losing its implementer. You are emerging a sure victor with all the spoil. I cancel every contract signed that linked you to lack, confusion, poverty, fear, disease and death. I break that umbilical code that linked you to the kingdom of the enemy. Your faith is triumphing and yes, you are marching forward!

Day 10

And after eight days again his disciples were within, and Thomas with them: then came Jesus, the doors being shut, and stood in the midst, and said, Peace be unto you.

(John 20:26 KJV)

They had shut the doors to ensure no one came in from outside. There were too many pressures, Jesus had just died and the memories of the cross were still fresh in their minds. They could be next on the line of death if they were not careful.

Jesus came in, the doors being shut and stood with them! What a glorious thing Jesus did on that day. If you only believe, you will see the glory of the Lord. He defied the power of locks and bolts. He defied doors and walked in! This is good news for you today. Ignore the doors that were locked as there is a capacity in you to walk through those doors as demonstrated by our Lord here. What we see the Master do we must also do. There are doors in your life that were stubbornly sealed; I want to emphasize today, WALK THROUGH THEM even in their state of closure! Don't wait for the day they will open. That door of disease that bolted you away from your health, walk through it, that door of poverty that kept you in fear and confusion, walk through it!

On His arrival, Jesus announced peace. He is the Man of Peace who brings order where chaos reigned. He imposes tranquility in situations of pandemonium. He will calm your storm today because you are a believer in His capability. At one time the disciples were panicking in the boat because of the storm which had arisen and they woke Jesus up. He spoke, "Peace be still," *(Matt 4:39)*. His all potent words resulted in the wind ceasing and so great was the serenity resulting. Jesus asked them why they were so fearful lacking faith. The presence of faith thwarts fear and doubt. It will cause the believer to be confident even when the situation seems unforgiving.

March forward today because you can! Chin high, chest out and hands in your pocket! The walls ahead are just a mirage when measured against the Word of God. The closed doors are just passing shadows. You carry inside you the One who defied the doors and walls, showing up in a place where others were locked away.

- **Declaration**

- I AM MARCHING FORWARD in Jesus' name! I walk through limitations without fear or doubt.

Day 11

And the earth was without form, and void; and darkness was upon the face of the deep. And the Spirit of God moved upon the face of the waters. And God said, Let there be light: and there was light.

(Gen 1:2-3 KJV)

God faced with formlessness, a barrenness of an earth and darkness, He refuses to acknowledge the state of things. Many would be terrified and look sideways, cry and blame somebody for the state. Not God, in Him everything begins and ends, Alpha and Omega!

His voice reverberated in the atmosphere, a voice of a commander demanding obedience and alignment. "LIGHT BE!" Words power filled, words faith filled demanding only compliance. Light immediately appeared, darkness cowered into nothingness.

"...God, who quickeneth the dead, and calleth those things which be not as though they were *(Rom 4:17 KJV)*." Abraham was acquainted with this God who makes reference to things that do not exist as if they did. He God is a Word God, not inclined to use His Words in vain and whatever He calls must COMPLY! Whether it is dead, it must hear His voice and come to life.

You child of God, made in His image and likeness are facing things that need your voice, words faith filled and power filled. That formlessness, barrenness and darkness facing your business, children, marriage and job await the voice of a commander. Don't make it worse by speaking about how bad the situation looks. Don't waste time speaking the state of affairs. There is a greater reality that the Word of God declared by your lips can bring.

Through faith today, call for a compliance of issues around you. Through words issue a warrant of arrest on that rampant poverty in your life. Through faith filled words you hold the key to the release of a whole generation tied by the chains of the evil one. Through words of faith spoken out of your mouth, things MUST

COMPLY! Don't cower back and surrender, UNLEASH words of power. Turn the tide using words.

- **Declaration**

- He gives life to the dead, I take God's style; I join Him in His way of doing things. I pronounce light in that darkness and see light taking over. I command order in the chaos and see the peace of God that passes all understanding manifest in my life.

Day 12

Being born again, not of corrupt-
ible seed, but of incorruptible, by
the word of God, which liveth and
abideth for ever.

(1 Pet 1:23 KJV)

The type of seed planted has within it the power to produce a nature. It carries the capacity
to carry the plant to different places and also
to the future. God's Word is an incorruptible
seed, one that never fails. It carries within it a
nature of victory.

You my friend were born again not of irresolute
seed but of this seed called the Word of God. It
has inside it the ability to make you what God
said you will be. It has the competence to put
you in health, power, riches and wealth. It has
the clout to turn the tide of fear in your life and
locate you for exploits.

This is the Word you must affirm as is! Collabo-
rate with the Word of God; speak it over your

life as it is. Don't twist it! Doing so means what you are vocalizing is twisted seed. It will fail to produce the correct results.

Be a sower of the Word, speak it in your spiritual field and you will be assured of a good harvest. Never let your mouth speak words that are vain. Never permit anything but the Word to depart from your lips. Death and life are in the power of the tongue. Jesus showed us that we can speak to a mountain and tell it to be removed and be positioned in another place as we march in faith. This is still true today saints, you can reposition things in your life using words coupled with faith. They fabricate explosions of valor proportions in the dominion of the spirit even the devil can't stand them.

- **Declaration**

- I change my job with words; I change any hopeless situation with words. I speak without fear or reservation. I map my life with words. I launch explosions in the devil's realm; I bamboozle him and his cohorts with words. The Word of God declared will not leave any stone unturned. It might seem like nothing has yet come to pass but just like any other seed, I give it time.

Day 13

There was a certain man there who had suffered with a deep-seated and lingering disorder for thirty-eight years.

(John 5:5 AMP)

Jesus' mission on earth was to do *good* things and at times He went off on His own just to bring joy to one soul. On one such day, He came to Bethesda, a place of uniqueness where the waters at the pool healed upon their stirring by an angel. Many with infirmities congregated there in anticipation of the day when they would be first in the pool.

A certain man was amongst them, thirty eight years of paralysis; a deep-seated and lingering disorder. Jesus without being told knew all about it. This man had hoped for long but had nobody to help him. He was at the threshold of a miracle all this time but was short of somebody to give him the final push. He was witness to many healings that took place, he could testify to those that came how this water healed upon the stirring of the angel.

As I write to you today, you are in a place where progress has eluded you. You try things and nothing seems to come through. You know that the things you are trying bring good results, you have testimonies of those who have done it and they succeeded. What you are lacking is that final push!

When Jesus approached this man, he changed his story and redefined his future. He would no longer sit by the pool but could now go and work for himself. He could go and be with his family. He could determine where to go and when to go there. What a glorious change of story!

As you move in faith, know that God Has better methods up his sleeve. Jesus did not need to put the man in the pool and call on the angel to come and stir the water or stir the water Himself since He had the power to do both. He spoke the Word, "Get up, pick up your bed and walk!" Strength came into his bones and his muscles; the man arose and picked up his bed. *"Thy words have upholden him that was falling, and thou hast strengthened the feeble knees,"* Job 4:4! The Word pronounced in faith

has power to re position the fallen. It is powerful enough to bring strength to those knees
that have been destroyed by arthritis.

- **Declaration**

- There is a testimony in the brew for me today! I let the Word permeate my being as I
  continue to declare it! Deep-seated lingering disorders are being turned into deep-
  seated lingering blessings!

Day 14

I, GOD, am doing the speaking. What I say happens. None of what I say is on hold. What I say, I'll do…

(Ezek 12:25 MSG)

When the Word of God is released, it carries with it colossal power to cause changes in any situation. Your part is to spice the Word with faith. This will make you a witness of that power bringing change anywhere. The same Word that preached to others didn't profit them because it was not mixed with faith in them that heard it **(Heb 4:2)**. All that great power was of no profit to them for lack of the ingredient of faith!

Today, the Word that God is speaking is not on hold, He is performing His whole Word. What He said concerning your victory is not on hold. Your victory is a reality today even in the face of that opposition. Your healing is real even in view of those symptoms. Delay will not clutter your life any more in this season. I am sent as a messenger to announce your release from the pain of stagnation. All you need to do is to unleash your faith in partnership with this Word. Shout I AM MOVING FORWARD!

The spirit of delay and stagnation had purposed to keep you in the confines of pain and lack. The Word of God is however commissioned with the capacity to sever everything that had pinned you down. Your life must take a whole new turn today because of the Word. The aspiration of God is for you to move forward, to relinquish an average life and leave a mark in this world. To raise sons and daughters that are God fearing and will carry through the legacy of faith.

"Is not my word like as a fire? saith the Lord; and like a hammer that breaketh the rock in pieces?" **(Jer 23:29 KJV)**. The Word is like a fire today, bringing a well needed warmth and heat where there was coldness and death. It is like a hammer breaking the rock in pieces. Every system of evil that had cemented itself in your life meets with its demise at the discharge of the Word of God today. Your advancement will be sure in this season as you let go of doubt and believe the Word.

- **Declaration**

- Healing is yours, joy is yours, peace that passes understanding is yours, success is yours! As the Word of God is enthroned in your life, every enemy of your soul is scattered in Jesus' name. 'Shout AMEN.'

detox

SECTION 3
TURN ON THE POWER

As believers, we have been given power and authority. It is critical that we turn on this power so we can live effectively. For the coming four days, we will focus on turning on this power.

Day 15

But ye shall receive power, after that the Holy Ghost is come upon you: and ye shall be witnesses unto me both in Jerusalem, and in all Judaea, and in Samaria, and unto the uttermost part of the earth.

(Acts 1:8 KJV)

Power in its many variations can mean many things. There is nothing as tragic as a lack of power where power must be applied. It is a blessing in any family to have at least one who has power. It is an opportunity to boast knowing that their matters can be solved quickly. Power can translate to financial power, political power, academic power and power of knowledge. We could also even look at mechanical power, electrical power and many other ways of its manifestation.

Well, in our family we are not just blessed with One who has power but this power has been passed on to all of us. Everything was happening too fast for the early Church. Just three years of effective ministry for Jesus. In that time when the disciples were just getting to know Him and understand His mission He was dead and hanging on the cross. After three days He was up and started appearing to them. It was a roller coaster of emotions! Before long He announced His departure to the ruffled disciples but here is the key..."You shall receive power..." This power is dunamis; it is force like the force of a huge army. A dynamic ability to cause changes!

His departure was technically an arrival on a large scale in the person of the Holy Spirit. The unleashing of the Holy Ghost into the world of believers, the very force and power of God! This only means believers should live a dynamic life! The army of heaven the Holy Spirit has come to dwell in those that receive Him! In the face of this power all other power wilts and surrenders.

This is the power that was on Samson when he picked the gates of a secure city and went uphill with them. This is the power that was on Peter when his shadow healed the sick in the streets. It is this power that was on Jesus Himself when He set free a man from a legion of demons.

This power that is beyond the analysis of man is on you today as His child. Do great things because you are powerful.

- **Declaration**

- I refuse to be bogged down by situations- any form of situation. I do not lack power in any area as I am equipped with the very force of heaven- it supersedes all the other forms of power available. I HAVE POWER!

Day 16

"...When he got to the vineyards of Timnah, a young lion came at him, roaring.

The Spirit of GOD came on him powerfully and he ripped it open barehanded, like tearing a young goat."

(Jdgs. 14:5-6 MSG)

When one is powered by the Spirit of God, he is capable of extra ordinary exploits. He approaches where others avoid, wins where others lose and he is courageous when those with the strength of the world cower.

Samson was just an ordinary guy but when the Spirit of the God came upon him, he did extra ordinary things. One of the days he was faced by a lion and it came at him roaring. It was an encounter that would have killed him. However, at that moment something extra ordinary happened, the Spirit of God came on him powerfully and he got hold of the lion and ripped it open with nothing is his hands. Here is the great thing, there was no tool or weapon in his hands; the Spirit upon him enhanced his capabilities and the strength of his hands. Making him some kind of superman capable of super things! He did it with no effort and the results were as if he tore a young goat.

Ordinary people can do extra ordinary things if they are driven by the Spirit of God. The greatest gift that God has given to the church is the person of the Holy Spirit to dwell in us. For the church of today, he does not visit as He did for Samson; He dwells in those that receive Him. We often fall short of exploits because we are not turning on the power that is inside us. When a computer is off, it is useless- it does not serve the purpose for which it was created. When you turn on the power, it will open for you a world of wonders. It will take you to places you never dreamed of. The Spirit of God is in you- turn on the power and be a witness of His wondrous deeds in your own life.

Turn on that power today to deal with the young lions that have surrounded your life. Deal with that lion of sickness, deal with that lion of poverty, deal with that lion of fear and death. Don't under utilise the power inside you. Shout I AM TURNING ON THE POWER!

- **Declaration**

- With the Spirit of God I am capable of great things. I live above the limitations that the world tried to impose on me. I go now; reap apart those mounting problems like I am ripping a young goat. The power is in me...!

Day 17

And one told David, saying, Ahithophel is among the conspirators with Absalom. And David said, O LORD, I pray thee, turn the counsel of Ahithophel into foolishness.

(2 Sam 15:31 KJV)

Power is not determined by the number of resources that are around you. It is never informed by the things you hold command over. David after being unseated by his own son Absalom had to run out of the kingdom without even shoes on his feet. Some of his most trusted officers were now with his enemies. He was privy to their counsel and knew the wisdom with which they operated.

What do you do when your influence over man is no longer effectual? When those who helped you build are after destroying everything you put together? They know where the main bolt is and where the central pillar lies. One move from them and you are doomed!

David shows us that the one associated with God wins, it does not matter who goes away from you, you will still wield power and influence on them. Ahithophel was a mighty counsellor. His counsel was like that of God. He never was wrong. When David heard that he had joined with his enemy, he used his access to a greater power. He called to the Lord, *"I pray thee, turn the counsel of Ahithophel into foolishness."*

This was the turning point! No matter how equipped Ahithophel was, he was not aligned with David, a man who was with God. His counsel would move from wisdom to foolishness. You might have been plundered of your resources. Your friends might have become your enemies. You might be looking like nobody but as a child of God, you can change things, you can turn them around. There is power available in you as you connect with the greatest power ever! When you can't move things, talk to God and He will move things on your behalf.

He will get into offices that you can't get into. He will speak where your voice is not heard. He will appear where you can't emerge. When you feel powerless, be assured right now that you are powerful.

- **Declaration**

- Today I silence all the Ahithophel's that counselled against you, plotting your death and destruction. I unleash the power of God to transport you back into your palace and throne. I declare mayhem and confusion in the enemy's camp. Shout, **LET'S TURN ON THE POWER!**

Day 18

"...That he may know ... what is the exceeding greatness of his power to us-ward who believe, according to the working of his mighty power,

Which he wrought in Christ, when he raised him from the dead, and set him at his own right hand in the heavenly places,"

(Eph 1:18-20 KJV)

When you believe in Jesus, there is power that you must get accustomed to. This is the power which God demonstrated when He raised Jesus from the dead and positioned Him on his right hand in the heavenly places. Picture this; it was a total silencing of the devil's antics. It was ultimate proof to the devil that he lacked capability to thwart the work of God. Though he had incited the death on the cross, it turned out he played into the great plan of God.

Upon Christ's resurrection, the devil could not do anything else but to peddle a lie that He was still dead. We know Jesus stayed around for forty or more days, this time He appeared to the disciples. He was not in a hurry to go to the Father and escape the tricks of the enemy. In this period, if the devil had power at all He would have done something just to take shame away from his camp. Resurrection itself was a powerful thing but this same power hauled Christ up and set him at the right hand of God in the heavenly places, a place which is far above all principalities, powers, dominions now and that to come! It is concluded that even in the future, the devil has been defeated!

Today you must know that you are not a small people! The One you have believed in wants you to know that you are now connected into miraculous power. He wants you to know that those challenges you were facing are small things compared to the power you are connected to. All you need to do is to **TURN ON THIS POWER!** Walk in this knowledge and you will see the challenges which looked like big and dominating mountains dwindling into small pebbles with no power to hold you back.

This exceeding, great power is directed towards you today to leave you a victor in all situations!

- **Declaration**

- I speak into your life today that this power will be evident in all you do. May those who hate you today realise that they are wasting their time. Promotion is yours today! You will be known in all the four corners of the earth. Make it count as you take advantage of this power. Shout **I WILL DO IT!**

detox

SECTION 4
POWER OF WORDS

Words are key; the Bible tells us 'death
and life are in power of the tongue.
Over the next nine days, we will deal
with words and release words of power in the spirit realm.

Day 19

No weapon that is formed against thee shall prosper; and every tongue that shall rise against thee in judgment thou shalt condemn. This is the heritage of the servants of the Lord, and their righteousness is of me, saith the Lord.

(Isa 54:17 KJV)

Words create, they build and with time they become real things. They are the foundation of everything manifest in the physical. God used words in creation. He fashioned this world using words. What is the significance of this to us as God's children?

In the spirit realm, there are weapons that are constantly fashioned against your life. The intention of the enemy has never been anything but your destruction, confusion, fear and death. He tries every tactic he can find to achieve this ultimate agenda. Today I want you to know that there is no weapon formed or fashioned against you that will prosper. This is a true word but you need to take charge to ensure that these weapons take no effect on your life. You have a duty to deal with every word that is raised against you.

This is how it works, when words are spoken, some that you hear and others you don't, you stand in a place where you must exercise authority over these words. To destroy them before they take effect and root. For words are like seeds that will germinate into plants and if they are negative judgments, they will bring a life of hardship and pain. You fight words with words, you must therefore rise up with decrees of your own, speaking in agreement with the Word of God. Uprooting all words of discord in the realm of the spirit that are operating against you!

You have the responsibility to speak into your own life. Don't look for pity from people and position your life for failure through negatively positioning yourself with your words. Today you will declare your own promotion, your own increase, your own joy and your own success. No one will do this for you but yourself. Indeed not a single weapon will prosper as you rise

69

to condemn every word that is raised against you in judgment. The power has been put into mouth to ensure that you fortify the walls of your life.

It is your responsibility to ensure your success. God has done everything that He must for your victory and success; it is left to you to maintain these using your mouth and words. You will succeed in this season! Heaven has conspired to ensure you make it!

- **Declaration**

- I maintain my victory today using words. I refuse to fear and I refuse to be intimidated. I am a master in my own right and I take charge over circumstances.

Day 20

And GOD said, "Good eyes! I'm sticking with you. I'll make every word I give you come true."

(Jer 1:12 KJV)

Every word that God speaks is effective and powerful. He will not let it come back to Him without finishing its designated task. There is a word on your life and today, you must join God in the fulfilment of that word.

Words are building blocks, capable of putting together whatever you desire. God used words in creation. Your victory has always been in your mouth. When you start speaking as God speaks, you will see the same results that God sees.

Don't give impetus to the negative things around you by speaking them. Don't glorify that poverty by letting it paint the walls of your heart with its effect such that your words become poverty only. Draw words of power from the Word of God and speak those words. Don't let that disease break you inside transforming your words into words of death. Refuse to agree with the work of the enemy using your mouth. Raise your levels by declaring words of power!

God has given you the power to create things and it is in your mouth. *The word is nigh thee even in your mouth* **(Rom 10:8)**. Never let your mouth go on a rampage speaking the wrong things. God is watching over his word to perform it, He will make His Word come true. It is therefore not wisdom to declare and speak the circumstances! Wisdom is speaking the word of God even in the situations you face. People might think you are mad but better for them to think that rather than for them to attend your funeral. The wrong words can kill faster than leprosy. Job's wife said to Job, *"Curse God and die* **(Job 2:9)**." She knew he would die faster than the time the leprosy he was languishing in would take to kill him.

Today, change your speaking regime! Declare words of power.

- **Declaration**

- I am the healed of God, poverty is not my portion, my marriage is a wonder, and fear is not my portion. I let all types of good words proceed out my mouth and begin to build myself up for a victorious life.

Day 21

A man's belly shall be satisfied with the fruit of his mouth; and with the increase of his lips shall he be filled.

Death and life are in the power of the tongue: and they that love it shall eat the fruit thereof.

(Pro 18:20-21 KJV)

Has it ever occurred to you that out of all creation, it is humans that are given the ability to speak? Languages may differ but speech remains a unique capability. The ability to speak and communicate has brought about development and a civilization that other creatures must envy.

Words are triggers in the spirit realm. They set in motion things that become big. The mouth is a small trigger which boasts of big results. It is the most productive member capable of bringing fulfilment to all the other members of the body. It wields the power of increase; out of it one can acquire substance. On the reverse, it can be a source of bitter waters issuing only death to the whole body and those around.

The devil was defeated and has no power; he will only be effective if he works together with you. One of the ways is to get you to speak words, manipulate the creative power already in you and bring about his agenda in your life.

Today, deploy a guard over your mouth. Hold on to your confession of faith! Raise words of victory from your mouth. For as long as you live, do not entertain some words on your mouth. The world is surprised about the amount of decay in the younger citizens and they wonder why? Listen to their music, they can't sing along to "I am bad!" and remain good. If the devil can put it in your ear, it's in your mind and then in your mouth, the cycle is complete. They can't sing along to Britney Spear's *Femme Fatale* and retain sexual integrity. They can't sing along to Gaga's *Judas* and continue to esteem Christ as king in their lives.

Today, take charge of the words that proceed out of your mouth. Death and life are in the power of the tongue.

- **Declaration**

- I CHOOSE LIFE today! I deploy a guard over my life to get rid of every wrong word.

Day 22

A wholesome tongue is a tree of life: but perverseness therein is a breach in the spirit.

(Pro 15:4 KJV)

Today I am a witness to the things that I spoke years ago. My words have taken root and become plants bearing fruit. Words will secure the future for you or destroy it. They are a weapon of mass destruction in the wrong hands.

The tongue that speaks good words is a tree of life. Very few references are given to the tree of life in the Bible after the book of Genesis. **Proverbs 15:4** is one of those few. A wholesome tongue is a tongue with curative power. Kind words will destroy the power of disease and sickness but the wrong words will obliterate a happy soul.

Perverseness in the tongue is a breach in the spirit. A breach is a cause for alarm because it means things are not operating as they should.

Something has been violated. You seem to be getting away with speaking the wrong words right now but be careful, it is matter of time. You are planting a big tree of death which you will not be able to uproot in the future.

Apostle James calls the tongue *a little member* boasting great things *(James 3:5)*. A little fire kindles a great matter. It can set on fire a great forest. Such is the tongue; it can ignite a level of matters never imagined. You rise and fall is in your tongue, your promotion or demotion, your prosperity or poverty is there on your tongue. What do you want today? Choose!

Take charge of the little member. Just as you control all the other members of your body at will, control the tongue. Break its liberty to speak the wrong things. Instead, find for it a regime of words that will bring about a tree of life for you; words that will secure your future! Let the fire that your own tongue starts be a fire for warmth, heat and that is used for good things. Fire is good, but when it's not controlled it is devastating.

- **Declaration**

- I LIGHT GOOD FIRES WITH MY TONGUE today! As I speak, I will witness the things
  I have spoken come to life through my
  words.

Day 23

Post a guard at my mouth, GOD, set a watch at the door of my lips.

(Psa 141:3 MSG)

Words are responsible for all we see, the good and the ugly! Your life is turned with words and irresponsible and senseless chatter results in the crumbling of your world. Irresponsibility with the tongue brings one into a place of regret where you are surprised as to where such big destruction sneaked into your life from.

You hold the power to create and that works via your mouth. The Psalmist cried to God and said, *post a guard at my mouth, set a watch at the door of my lips.* He realised that he often was a partaker of the words that he spoke. His words yielded a harvest for him. He needed a discipline and external help to monitor the words of his mouth.

This is the thing child of God; you win and fall on your lips. With your mouth you design the world that you want to live in. Houses are built by words, health is a result of words and prosperity is words. You choose today what you want. *Death and life are truly in the power of the tongue (Pro 18:21)*. You are the one who must choose what you want.

Every idle word will be called to judgment so challenge yourself to make every word that you speak a good word. **Hosea 14:2** tells us, take with you words and turn to the Lord. It is words that bring a turnaround in your life. Is a storm brewing in your job? Take words. Is it a marriage that is on the edge? Take words. Is it a business that is struggling? Take words. Hold on to your confession of faith. Soon this thing will turn in obedience to the words of your mouth- so make the words good, without wavering, hold on to your confession.

We know the enemy is a defeated foe; he will not be able to withstand a good regime of words. He will have to flee as words are the ultimate resistance. Even when your tongue cannot utter words, let them reverberate in your mind as you declare the victory already attained on your behalf.

- **Declaration**

- I am winning. I am rising above the storms of life, propelled higher and higher by the words of my mouth. I prophesy into my life- the joy of the Holy Ghost and the victory of Christ is mine.

Day 24

Thou shalt also decree a thing, and it shall be established unto thee: and the light shall shine upon thy ways.

When men are cast down, then thou shalt say, There is lifting up; and he shall save the humble person.

(Job 22:28-29 KJV)

Decrees are authoritative orders that have the force of law. Today, we issue these orders and we will see their establishment in your life. Let these words raise you up from your point of weakness and supply your needs in every area.

I decree today that your body is in health. I speak to every bone, vein and every vessel. It will operate the way God created it. As it was in the beginning, I decree it will be so with you. We remove every foreign object, growth, interference and release you into a life of divine health.

I decree today that prosperity is your portion. As the Word has said, Beloved, *I wish above all things that thou mayest prosper and be in health, even as thy soul prospereth.* **(3 John 1:2)**. I decree that your advancement will be evident to all. They will see the glory of the Lord on your life. As Abraham started from nothing and became great, as Isaac was in a land of famine and started from nothing and became great- I decree today that greatness is your portion.

I decree, fear is vanquished in your life. Faith has become your way of functioning. Fear has no hold on you anymore. You will do exploits through faith in this season.

I decree, the power of toil is broken in your life. You will not go around in circles. Like Elisha who said to Elijah, I will not remain in Gilgal (a circle of stones) but I will move forward with you. I decree that whatever you begin will move to a place of fruitfulness.

I decree today, that those that were raiding you, stealing from you and stabbing you from behind are exposed. You will see the goodness of the Lord in the land of the living. The Lord will send you the right people to congregate with

84

you. He will send you the right employees, and He will send you those who celebrate you.

I decree today, open doors in your life- even those doors that were rusting because they would not open for you. I decree them open and command them to let go of their stubbornness.

I decree today, every altar raised against you destroyed and split in pieces. I decree the adjudicators of such altars are developing withered hands prohibiting them from reaching you for harm.

- **Declaration**

- I decree that you are coming out, and you are coming out strong.

Day 25

*Behold, I and the children whom the LORD hath given me **are** for signs and for wonders in Israel from the LORD of hosts, which dwelleth in mount Zion.*

(Isa 8:18 KJV)

This is my decree over you! You are for signs and you are for wonders. Your life is beautified for this season to bring glory to God. You are a new creature, the righteousness of God through Christ. You are begotten of the Father, a world over-comer of our time **(1 John 5:1-4)**. You are a master because God has given you mastery over demonic spirits. You reign through life; the eternal life which is at work in you has made you a dominant being.

You are what God says you are; you can do what He says you can do. He will do in you all that He did in Christ for you. You have God's nature in you- His love nature, His creative nature and His faith nature. If God is for you, nobody can be against you. In this season, you will triumph over every bother in your life.

He is the vine and you are the branch. You draw nourishment from Him. You feed from Him; you are connected to the same system as Him. Your hands are the medium through which life pours. You are living the abundant life. His words broke the power of death; your words have the same power. As you speak His word, it is having the same effect coming out of your lips.

You no longer have cares, anxieties and burdens. Cast them all upon Him because He cares *(1 Pet 5:7)*. The Lord is your shepherd, you shall not want: you do not want for money, you do not want for health or rest. You don't lack strength, He is all you need. This is a living reality. My God shall supply all your need according to His riches in glory *(Phil 4:19)*.

Every disease, every weakness and every infirmity was laid on Jesus Christ on the cross and you are free from them. You are in Christ Jesus who was made to you wisdom, righteousness, sanctification and redemption *(1 Co 1:30)*. You have God's nature in you, His very life is operative in you, don't let this life lie dormant!

Yes, you can do all things through Christ that enables you and gives you strength. He is your ability and sufficiency. He is your perfect redemption from weakness, fear and lack. You stand complete in Him, a victor over all your enemies.

- **Declaration**

- Thanks be to God who always leads me in triumph in every place. All things are possible to me because I believe. It is no longer I that live but Christ that lives in me. THIS IS MY PORTION!

Day 26

"…he shall have whatsoever he saith. Therefore I say unto you, what things soever ye desire, when ye pray, believe that ye receive them, and ye shall have them."

(Mark 11:23-24 KJV)

What you say is what you get. Your mouth is strategically located for the acquisition and determination of the kind of life you will have. Truth is a stabilizing force and the Word of God is truth. God has said to us we will have what we say but many believers keep saying what they have. They get surprised when their portion is nowhere near what the word says.

Today, you must turn away the tide of fear, lack, poverty, death, confusion, sickness and stress with words. Declarations that come out of your spirit man:

Behold I am in Christ, I am a new creature: old things are passed away, behold all things have become new *(2 Cor 5:17)*. I do not fear the past and I am not afraid of what tomorrow holds. I am an heir of God, joint heir with Christ there is nothing that I will fear for my inheritance is of the Father and it is secure *(Rom 8:17)*. The power of God is in me to put me over; greater is he that's in me than he that is in the world *(1 John 4:4)*. I am quickened according to the word of God. I thank God that the ability of God is released within me. I overcome every obstacle, trial and challenge that comes my way.

Thank God the wealth of the sinner is laid up for the just. I thank God I am the just and I will get my part by acting on the Word of God *(Pro 13:22)*. My prosperity is sure, physically, spiritually and financially as 3 John verse 2 says, *"Beloved, I wish above all things that you mayest prosper and be in health, even as thy soul prospereth."* No weapon formed against me shall prosper, but whatsoever I do will prosper *(Isa 54:17)*. God is perfecting that which concerns me. I declare that favour is pursuing me and finding me. I see perfection in every area of my life.

This is a new beginning, the dawning of a new era. Whatever I am touching with my hands to do is prospering. Fear has lost its grip over me,

I am arising in the confidence that faith gives. Like Joshua, I am winning wars, like Elijah, I am calling for fire from the heaven and my prayers are answered. Like Paul, I am moving in the mighty and power of the Holy Spirit. Like Peter, I am seeing wonders performed even by my shadow.

- **Declaration**

- I decree, my days of fear, suffering, stagnancy and poverty are over.

Day 27

*Hereby perceive we the love **of God**, because he laid down his life for us: and we ought to lay down **our** lives for the brethren.*

(1 John 3:16 KJV)

To perceive is to go beyond sight, to see things with your spirit. Some were accused of seeing without perception **(Mark 4:12)**. For the early church, the Word 'perceive' became part of their vocabulary. They would not trust the things their eyes saw but the things their spirits perceived. Perception taps into revelation knowledge not natural knowledge.

In **Joshua 22:31**, Phinehas says, *"This day we perceive that the Lord is amongst us."* What their natural eyes could not see, their spirits were in full sight of. The Shunamite woman upon seeing the prophet Elisha said, *"I perceive this is a holy man of God which passeth by us continually **(2 Ki 4:9)**."* Many saw the prophet, many knew he was a man of God but they did not take the next step because they never came to the position of perception- seeing with the spirit.

Jesus said to the disciples as they reasoned concerning bread, *"Perceive ye not yet... having eyes see ye not?"* **(Mark 8:17-18)**. After all the spiritual training, Jesus expected the disciples to be on another level of perception. When the woman with the issue of blood touched the hem of Jesus' garment, He did not see her but He perceived, *"Somebody hath touched me: for I perceive that virtue is gone out of me* **(Mark 8:46).**

Our declarations today are therefore declarations of perception, the things that we see with our spirits:

Declare today, I perceive, that ancient doors that were closed in my life are opening at the command of my voice. Doors that had become restrictions to my progress are submitting to me. I AM GRATEFUL!

I perceive that riches and honor are coming to me. The lack of yesterday is diminishing in the light of the greatness ahead of me. I AM ENCOURAGED!

I perceive that every weapon that was fashioned and manufactured against me is failing in its purpose. I am emerging the victor in all situations that I am facing. I AM A WINNER!

I perceive that the shout of the King is in my life today. As I go I witness victories without number. VICTORY IS MINE!

I perceive that an angel outpost has been deployed on my behalf. To fight on my behalf and register victories on my behalf! For His angels hearken to the Word of His command. I AM PROTECTED!

- **Declaration**

- I pray for you, that the shackles of toil be broken off your life. That you move from oppression to freedom, from repression to peace and from suppression to joy. May you be the one giving a testimony this week.

detox

SECTION 5
GROW IN KNOWLEDGE

Understanding who you are goes a long way in taking you forward in your walk as a believer. In the coming days, we deal with understanding and knowing your identity.

Day 28

I lifted up mine eyes again, and looked, and behold a man with a measuring line in his hand.

Then said I, Whither goest thou? And he said unto me, to measure Jerusalem, to see what is the breadth thereof, and what is the length thereof. And, behold, the angel that talked with me went forth, and another angel went out to meet him, And said unto him, Run, speak to this young man, saying, Jerusalem shall be inhabited as towns without walls for the multitude of men and cattle therein:

(Zec 2:1-4 KJV)

Why is it that you can have people of the same origin, same education, same background but different levels of success in life? People of the same age who are miles apart in terms of their achievements? These are some of the questions that started running in my mind. The Spirit of the Lord then dropped these three words in my heart, DIMENSIONS, LEVELS and MEASUREMENTS. I then perceived that there are measures that are available. Ways to move from one step to another, methods to transform one's life from mediocrity to excellence, poverty to wealth, weakness to power and failure to success.

As the prophet Zechariah lifted his eyes, he saw a man with a measuring line in his hand. He asked him what his destination was. His answer was simple; he was going to measure Jerusalem. He wanted to know how big the city was. What transpires thereafter is interesting. The angel that was with the prophet meets with another angel and instructs that angel to RUN and bring a message to this young man. Shout WHEN ANGELS RUN! Angels are fast already but when they bear an instruction to run, it means that there are urgent messages that must be delivered. I see angels running on your behalf today, bearing special tidings for your life.

The message was simple but powerful, JERUSALEM SHALL BE INHABITED AS TOWNS WITHOUT WALLS. It was going to be a city full of people and cattle. Today, you are the Jerusalem of

God. His city within which He has chosen to dwell! He lives in you and his BIG IDEA is that you be a city without limits. In God's eyes, you are a city loaded with all the good things. In His eyes, you are a success, free from limiting disease and poverty. Free from death and disability. Free from confusion and fear. Free from marital strife and pain. You are a city of no limits, a city prosperous function at the TOP LEVEL. Shout THAT'S ME!

- **Declaration**

- I cannot be measured because God dwells in me. There are higher levels that are meant for me. Dimensions of dynamic proportions are my portion. My levels from now on are TOP NOTCH!

Day 29

So this Daniel prospered in the reign of Darius, and in the reign of Cyrus the Persian.

(Dan 6:28 KJV)

God has set levels for you, it a path of righteousness where there is life. When opposition comes your way, don't despair. All attempts of this world to put you down will meet with revenge from their own system.

Laws were crafted to stop Daniel's move to the next level. An attempt to block his promotion came with disastrous consequences for those who did it. They ended up being eaten by the lions.

Whenever Daniel went down, he came back for a higher level. His dimensions remained in shift mode to ensure a fulfilment of every Word God spoke upon his life. Daniel prospered in the reign of two kings. You child of God will see the hand of God in this season. The political system has no power to keep you down. Your detractors only try to put you down at their peril. The devil is a defeated foe and anything designed to kill you is becoming your stepping stone to higher ground!

Daniel was well positioned in his prayer life. The enemy knew an attack on this would spell a slowing down of his progress. There is no decree that will stop the power of prayer. Let it be clear to you right now friend that the imposing mountains that were before you have no power to limit you. You can rise above them because you are God's Jerusalem. In every sphere, your levels will meet with no limits. Shout THAT'S ME!

The lions that were so keen for a meal that day lost their appetite because of Daniel. I see poverty losing its appetite over you. I see marauding demonic forces that have bothered your blood line for decades without end losing their appetite over you and your family. I see you rising above disease, fear, death, confusion and all sorts of evil that was designed against you by the enemy. You will have your levels and you will have them now. Shout GIVE ME MY LEVELS!

- **Declaration**

- Promotion is yours, joy is yours, success is yours, and prosperity is your portion. We send a Word on assignment today to change your dimensions lift your levels and enlarge your measures! You are a testimony going somewhere. Refuse to be discouraged, keep your eyes on Him who begun a good work in you and will finish it. Shout AMEN!

Day 30

Therefore God give thee of the dew of heaven, and the fatness of the earth, and plenty of corn and wine:

Let people serve thee, and nations bow down to thee: be lord over thy brethren, and let thy mother's sons bow down to thee: cursed be every one that curseth thee, and blessed be he that blesseth thee.

(Gen 27:28-29 KJV)

When Jacob left his father's house, he left rushing, with nothing on him but only his walking stick and the blessing pronounced on him. It was this blessing that would ensure that he came back as two bands **(Gen 32:10)**. This blessing took him from zero to hero, from poverty to wealth and from defeat to victory.

When Jacob went to his uncle Laban, he became an employee to him, working for his wives first and then for his wealth. A few promises later of increases that never came, Jacob realised that his life was not changing. He remained in the same place despite all the hard work he was putting in. There was a need for new methods otherwise he would reach retirement age with nothing.

I want you to know that the blessing on him started working the day he was prayed for by his father Isaac. Many miss it in that they don't understand the grace already abounding and at work in their lives. Those around them see it and they manipulate that blessing to their maximum benefit. For Laban, there was a change of fortunes when Jacob took over. His money increased, his cattle increased, losses were eradicated! Only profit was the order of his business. Laban even visited his witchdoctors to ask why he was doing so well. He was told the reason was Jacob and all costs he had to make sure he stayed.

One day Jacob woke up and demanded his LEVELS. He protested the order of things. He realised that he was getting no reward for the work he was doing. It was a demand for a change of levels. A demand to be shifted from where he was to where he should have been!

104

In your life, develop a discernment of what the Spirit is saying. Never settle for less at times when you can have more. Never be satisfied with things as they are, there is a better place for you! When you settle, stagnation sets in and death of dreams is imminent. I declare a resurrection of your dreams today. Shout THAT'S ME!

- **Declaration**

- I demand a new position in every place that you I am. I demand my promotion; I issue a summary judgment against my limitations. GIVE ME MY LEVELS!

Day 31

And when he came to himself, he said, How many hired servants of my father's have bread enough and to spare, and I perish with hunger!

(Luke 15:17 KJV)

Jacob came to a place where he realized that his LEVELS were being undermined by Laban. He wanted to work for his family and build wealth that would go on to the seventh generation. It was a wake- up call- a call to break the bondage that binds many through-out life today.

Like Jacob, the prodigal son had grown up in desirable circumstances. Unlike Jacob, this young man was uncouth and uncultured. Spoiled to the core, he asked his father one day to give him his inheritance. It was divided for him and he took a journey to a faraway country. There he lived like a fool- spending it all as a man with no principles. Wealth unman-aged depletes. It flies away like a bird!

A great famine fell upon the land and young man came into want. He was out completely. He went from hero to zero, from something to nothing, from somebody to nobody. That day he was like the devil after being kicked out of heaven, the glory stripped off him. There were no jobs available for him. Nobody could employ him, he was spoiled. The only thing he could put on his CV was- drinking, dancing, spending money etc. One man took him, gave him a very low level job with the pigs. "Feed them, clean them and eat their leftovers," he said. That was the place he landed- the level of pigs.

He took the job, worked as hard as he could. There was no increase, no promotion and no progress! The only thing that was changing was his self esteem, it was his health, and it was his self confidence. One day, he began to THINK, "... *he came to himself.*" This is not me, my father has many servants and they have too much food and I am going hungry everyday! These are not my LEVELS! I was created for dominion, I was made to rule! There is a BLESSING resting on my life. He shouted GIVE ME MY REAL LEVELS...!

Child of God, see what you have become? See the levels man have given you? They have been trying to measure you and classify you all along! Wake up from your slumber. Today is the day you must say I CAN'T BE MEASURED.

They don't know what's in you, that is why they put you with the pigs! They have no idea who your father is. I challenge you to come to yourself today and shout GIVE ME MY LEVELS!

- **Declaration**

- Health is mine, wealth is mine, peace is mine, and joy is mine!

Day 32

And the flocks conceived before the rods, and brought forth cattle ringstraked, speckled, and spotted. And Jacob did separate the lambs, and set the faces of the flocks toward the ringstraked, and all the brown in the flock of Laban; and he put his own flocks by themselves, and put them not unto Laban's cattle.

(Gen 30:39-40 KJV)

Whilst scientists are still to understand how genetics work, Jacob the patriarch had already delved into this science which still baffles many. King Solomon rightfully declares *there is nothing new under the sun* **(Ecc 1:9)**. How does one change his circumstances? How do you move from one level to the next? Today, I boldly declare that whatever it is that has been pulling you back can be altered and changed- even if it's encoded in your DNA. If the disease is in your DNA today, you can turn

109

it around. If that poverty is in your DNA you can turn things around and I can prove it!

When Jacob passed through Laban's flock, he took out everything that was speckled and spotted and put a three days journey between them and the rest of Laban's sheep. He was left with flocks that had no genes to produce spotted and speckled. Whatever he would do, it needed something that would go to the core of the genetic makeup of the livestock he was dealing with. No stress for Jacob, he knew a God who had put the blessing on his life. He knew something called the GOD FACTOR that has no respect for things that are called impossible by man.

Like an expert, Jacob did the unusual, he took streaks of white and brown that he made from green rods and placed them in front of the livestock as they conceived. He made them look at what he wanted and his faith was connected to that. His secret was not in the type of tree he chose but in the faith he exercised. When the best and the strong were to give birth, he brought them in front of this creation of his and they gave him the spotted and the speckled. When the weak and frail were to conceive, he took them far away from his creation and they gave birth to Laban's next generation of

110

flocks. His best ideas and his best sweat now towards his own signature wealth! The blessing was now at full work in his own house.

You have freedom of CHOICE! Jacob made the call on which animal gave birth to what he wanted! The scientists say that spots and speckles on animals is a *rare mutation of the colour gene*. For Jacob, he made a rare mutation a common mutation.

- **Declaration**

- If wealth was rare in your life and family, I declare that through faith, it is becoming common in your life. If health was rare, I declare a commonality in your life like never before. Your faith is going to the core of your story! Your life will no longer be interjected with episodes of suffering and confusion. Laban will not keep you a slave to toy with when he wants! Shout THESE ARE MY MEASUREMENTS!

Day 33

"Judge not, that you may not be judged; for your own judgement will be dealt--and your own measure meted--to yourselves."

(Matt 7:1-2 WNT)

Jesus Christ, the greatest teacher ever reveals a grand principle here. You would rather not judge because the level you assign in your judgment is what you get back. It works like a boomerang. This principle does not only speak of relationships as many would shallowly perceive it but it goes deep into every aspect of life as a working principle.

"...and your own measure meted to yourself." This is *antimetreo*, measure in return. The level of commitment you give to something is the level of commitment you get back. You are standing as a judge through life and what you are willing to put in is what you are surely going to get back. It is a great investment scheme

that everybody participates in everyday with or without knowing. You give to take!

> "But he that is spiritual judgeth all things, yet he himself is judged of no man."
>
> **(1 Co 2:15 KJV.)**

When one is spiritually attune, they judge with greater depth and the response they get is of great depth. They measure with access to the greatest intellect ever, the mind of Christ. All things stand to be judged by you, it is a process of scrutinizing, investigating, interrogating, determining, examining and searching. Before you give up or surrender, have you fully judged the situation? Have you fully measured it? There has to be a way in it all, if your judging is shallow and not informed by the Spirit, you let go of opportunities that would have changed your life going forward.

There are things you must revisit today, cases you must reopen, ideas you trashed that must come afore. These must be awarded the opportunity of a fair measurement.

The system of the world was never designed for cry babies. The devil himself takes no prisoners, he comes only to *kill, steal and destroy (John 10:10)*. Never to nurse, never to feel pity! Progress is only for those who will say GIVE ME MY REAL LEVELS!

These levels are informed by your measurements (*judging*), the very principles that inform your life, your work culture, your relationships, your faithfulness to yourself and to others. Remember all this is coming back to you like a boomerang so you might as well do it right.

Input determines output! For any positive action there is a positive result coming. Any negative action, be on the lookout for the revenge. Today, calibrate your measurements to the greatest intellect ever, the mind of Christ.

• **Declaration**

• I bind every force stealing your progress. I bind every force responsible for delay in your life. I say march forward in the power of the Spirit. Ignore every opposing voice, you are a winner today. Shout I RECEIVE!

SECTION 6
YOUR BILL OF RIGHTS

In life, it is important to know your rights. In the next days, we deal with your rights as a child of God.

Day 34

I will ransom them from the power of the grave; I will redeem them from death: O death, I will be thy plagues; O grave, I will be thy destruction: repentance shall be hid from mine eyes.

(Hosea 13:14 KJV)

Every affliction of the enemy has an expiration date and today I announce that every affliction of the enemy in your life must expire. May the power of Jehovah lift you up into your special space! Where sorrow can't afflict you, where fear can't harass you and where confusion can't torment you.

I declare you watched and protected! The grave can't hold you anymore. We know that our Lord and saviour is risen from the grave, it could not hold nor keep him captive. When the time of release came, the stone was rolled away and He emerged triumphant. You too must arise from every situation that threatened

116

you and roped you in bondage. Jesus came as a ransom from the power of the grave. Death can't keep you a slave through its agents of disease and pain. I declare you are ransomed today from the power of sickness.

- **As scripture declares:**

    O death, where is thy sting? O grave, where is thy victory?

    1Co 15:55 (KJV)

May you walk as an agent of heaven! Free from sorrow, pain, disease, confusion and fear. May the world see the ransoming power of the father manifest in your life! May you in turn be an agent of this healing, an ambassador of this life that you have received.

His death on the cross freed you from any form of bondage. His resurrection brought justification in your life. You qualify for a new life- a life of victory and triumph. He died so that you may live. He lives so you may stand as a commander in this life.

Stand strong in whatever you do knowing the price for your victory was paid. Refuse to settle

for less in this life. Don't let the enemy nego-
tiate you out of the best. Anything from him
however small has no right to stand in your life.

Health is yours, prosperity is yours, joy is yours,
progress is yours, and power is yours! All good
things are yours and today they must manifest
in your life, family, business and job. Whatever
you touch with your hands to do is blessed!
Stand I say, stand strong in your rights as a
child of God.

As you come to awareness of your rights as a
child of God, the devil must flee your life! Take
nothing less; He died so you may live.

- **Declaration**

- I command supernatural solutions to your
  natural problems today. I declare that your
  enemies will walk away disappointed and
  you will emerge victorious in every situation. Say I AGREE!

Day 35

Christ hath redeemed us from the curse of the law, being made a curse for us: for it is written, Cursed is every one that hangeth on a tree:

That the blessing of Abraham might come on the Gentiles through Jesus Christ; that we might receive the promise of the Spirit through faith.

(Gal 3:13-14 KJV)

The curse was upon us, designed to keep us in poverty, sickness and spiritual death. We were prisoners destined for eternal devastation! The redeemer, Christ broke the power of this being made a curse for us. The law was clear, *"cursed is everyone that hangs on a tree."* Everything that was designed to keep you captive, every instrument that was designed for you to hang on was destroyed that day on the cross. Say AMEN.

As He broke the curse by being made a curse, He released the blessing of Abraham on the Gentiles. Gateways were opened that day for all who believe to march into an inheritance. The blessing now rests on you child of God! Never let the deception of the deceiver hoodwink you out of what belongs to you through his lies.

Stand in faith today, walk in the fullness of the Holy Spirit through faith! As you do so, the Holy Spirit, the power of God will cause you to be a witness of miracles without number. Every family, generational, marriage, business or whatever nature of curse is broken! No curse can and will rule over you because the work of the redeemer was fully accomplished.

Today, claim your rights as a child of God. Refuse to walk in ignorance as to what your inheritance contains. Don't accept a low level of life just because the majority have done so. Rise to new levels of power, wealth and spiritual accomplishments. Turn the tide around in your family, business, community and nation by claiming everything that was done for us on the cross by Christ Jesus.

- **Declaration**

- Christ has redeemed me from the curse of the law- I am above poverty, sickness and spiritual death. The blessing of Abraham now rests on me. I am a winner wherever I am. I refuse to be a partaker of anything that is not in line with this blessing. I am the blessed and not the cursed in Jesus' name.

detox

SECTION 7
YOU ARE A COMMANDER

In this 40 day journey, you must come to the realisation that you are a commander of the supernatural. As a child of God, this is the place you have been given. You must take this place of authority.

Day 36

And God said, Let us make man in our image, after our likeness: and let them have dominion over the fish of the sea, and over the fowl of the air, and over the cattle, and over all the earth, and over every creeping thing that creepeth upon the earth.

(Gen 1:26 KJV)

In God's order of creation, you were never designed to be ordinary. When He made man, his role was to dominate creation and carry the image and likeness of God. His role must be that of a commander or a captain to spear head God's agenda here on earth.

As God's child, you are a spiritual being in his order, your place is that of authority over all kinds of situations. One day, Jesus called the twelve and gave them power against unclean spirits to cast them out and to heal all manner of sickness (Matt 10:1). The word power here means authority, force or capacity. As the disciples went, they experienced the working of this power in the reversal of evil that the enemy was doing through demonic spirits.

Jesus went about doing good, healing all those that were oppressed of the devil (Acts 10:38). He tells us that those who believe in Him are capable of doing the works he did and even greater works (John 14:12). Believers were left with a mandate here on earth to bring order and to maintain Christ's victory.

Child of God, understand today that yours should be the role of a commander. You must command the supernatural here on earth. There is not one thing of the enemy that must take charge over your life. You must walk in the authority that has been given to believers. As you walk in this authority, you are one to liberate others from the oppression of the enemy.

- **Declaration**

- Today, may the supernatural be your order of life. May you be a witness of God's
power and authority here on earth! There
is grace on your life to command things
and as you do so, may situations obey
your voice. I see alignment coming in every area of your life, in your health, family,
ministry and finances. Victories are yours
today as you act in your place of authority. Say AMEN!

Day 37

And Jesus rebuked him, saying, Hold thy peace, and come out of him. And when the devil had thrown him in the midst, he came out of him, and hurt him not.

And they were all amazed, and spake among themselves, saying, What a word is this! for with authority and power he commandeth the unclean spirits, and they come out.

(Luk 4:35-36 KJV)

Years back we embarked on an evangelism outreach into rural Mozambique. The area we went into was riddled with poverty after the war. One of the things we encountered was the clear demonic presence and activity in the area. As we preached in this place, we ended up confronting a witch doctor who kept opposing the work we were doing. When we got to her shrine, we preached the word to her and began to pray and the demons in her began to manifest. They started speaking through her, saying they would not go away because all that the woman had in her homestead was their work. They were the ones that had given her the livestock and the home. In authority given to us, we prevailed against every demonic force that was at work in the area.

Jesus' work here on earth demonstrates to us the role of a commander. He held authority over demonic spirits and they obeyed his voice. The work of the devil on earth is to kill, steal and destroy **(John 10:10)**. Wherever you see destruction and hurt, there is one who is responsible; his name is Satan and his cohorts. In authority and power Jesus addressed the activities of the devil.

His words were words of power. Anointed words to bring change and a difference! When he spoke, there had to be alignment of issues. The man had had an unclean devil in him and when he confronted Jesus, freedom came to him.

As you go through life and you come across challenges or issues that are overtly caused in the realm of the spirit, you must know that as a child of God you have been given authority and power to command issues.

Luke 10:19 tells us, "behold I give you power and authority to trample on serpents and scorpions, and all over the power of the enemy; and nothing shall by any means hurt you." We can operate as champions here on earth owing to the power and authority we have received. We can command the supernatural and emerge with victories without number.

- **Declaration**

- I pray for you today that you awaken and this power and authority you have been given to operate here on earth. I pray that challenges that faced you bow down to the words of your command. Declare today, I AM A COMMANDER!

Day 38

For the earnest expectation of the creature waiteth for the manifestation of the sons of God.

(Rom 8:19 KJV)

Ever been in a place of intense anticipation? Where you waited for something to happen or for something to be announced? Many times we have waited for results after a school year or any other tests with this kind of anticipation.

Creation is waiting! These are strong words. All creation is waiting for a certain release that must come. This release is the salvation of all creation. With anticipation every created thing looks forward to the manifestation of the sons of God. When the sons of God are disclosed, they bring answers to the questions all creation has been asking. Notice that there is no limit to the 'creatures', it is every created thing. Adam in the garden was an answer to the plant life, animal life, the fowls and the fish. His manifestation as a son in the garden meant that all creation could operate at their optimum capacity.

When the sons of God arise, they turn the unturned, they release the unreleased; they hire the un-hired and fire the un-fired! They bring a new order, the right order into all things.

These carry a certain nature. They are not afraid and they can't be intimidated. They know whom they have believed in and move in authority and power. They are a people of authority, led by the Spirit of God. Exploits are the order of their day and at their sight, devils withdraw!

The challenge is clear for you today; will you arise as a son of God? Will you bring answers to a struggling world around you or you will be content as just an ordinary child in the house of God? Will you dare the un-dared and operate in a rare order of faith? The world needs you and today you must break the routine and seek God in a new way. You came to this world carrying something unique. Don't waste time vilifying those that are doing something, show what's in you! Manifest as a son!

- **Declaration**

- I pray for you today, that something be stirred in you so you may see the demand creation is making on you to manifest. I pray that the Holy Spirit will empower you to become the special breed that you are. Truly the world has not seen anything yet. It's your turn to make the news. Shout I AM MANIFESTING!

DAY 39

*For as many as are led by the Spirit
of God, they are the sons of God.*

(Rom 8:14 KJV)

The Holy Spirit carries in Him the intentions of
God, His desires and His perfect will. He knows
the heart of God and is capable of transforming the one He leads into a perfect bearer of
God's heart on earth. We are all products of
the leadership that has had oversight on us.
Our leaders have impacted our lives in a great
way whether negative or positive.

Leadership of the Spirit of God makes one
a son of God, not just a son but a carrier of
the heart of God. He does not function in ac-
cordance with human emotions. He does not
follow the way of the world but is totally and
wholeheartedly committed to what God is doing.

God will entrust His power to the one that is
led and who is under the control of His Spirit.

132

If control is not there, abuse is imminent and creation will be punished by one who is meant to benefit it. The place of sonship is a place of surrendering your rights to the Holy Spirit. It is a place where you let go and let God take charge through His Spirit! It is a place where your heart is totally given to the Holy Spirit to take charge.

The Father's desire today is the arising of worth sons. Those that can carry the gospel with integrity and turn the tide of evil in society! The qualities of these sons are well expounded by the prophet Joel in Joel 2. They move with the fire of the Holy Spirit, they are fast like horses. They are not limited by challenges, they leap over mountains. They run like mighty men and climb over walls of limitation. They march forward without breaking rank and do not fight against each other. They are immune to injury when attacked.

The question remains, will you manifest as a son? Creation depends on you for a total change in the tide of evil. God put you here on earth to be an answer. This will be achieved through the Holy Spirit who has come to partner with us.

Break the routine today; refuse to follow the path of the whole world. Become a blessing by giving yourself wholly to the leadership of the Spirit.

- **Declaration**

- I pray for you today, that you arise in this day to bless the world. It doesn't matter what you have become today, your age does not matter, you can still turn around and make an impact.

Day 40

The secret things belong unto the Lord our God: but those things, which are revealed, belong unto us and to our children forever, that we may do all the words of this law.

(Deuteronomy 29:29 KJV)

There are many things that the world has not discovered. In as much as the human race has advanced technologically and in other aspects, there are still many hidden things that only God knows. The greatest gold mine is still unexplored and the most valuable diamond is not yet discovered.

The great prophet Moses touches on the subject of secrets which he rightly says belong to God. The things which are revealed belong to us and our children to cash on. Going back to the secret things, there are methods, formulas, treasures, means, medicines and solutions not yet discovered. These will be unlocked and revealed only to the genuine sons of God!

The Psalmist says,

> *The secret of the Lord is with them that fear him;*
>
> *and he will show them his covenant.*
>
> **(Psalm 25:14 KJV).**

Sons are custodians of secrets because of their heart that reverences God. Their hearts are in line with the heart of God and as a result they are not prone to abuse the revealed secrets. I believe in this season as the sons of God manifest (Rom 8:19), there is an unlocking and revealing of old age secrets.

As sons arise in different areas, secrets are being revealed to them. Those in field of medical research must expect new medicines to be revealed to them. Those in business must expect the creation of new products. Those in ministry must expect new types of miracles, signs and wonders. Those in engineering must get ready for the creation of new machines.

136

As the secrets are being revealed, things that were hard will become easy because of new methods of doing them.

The Spirit of The Lord is ever ready to raise you to another level. You will see God's hand in a new way. I pray for you, that as you walk with the Spirit of God in this season. May you see the hand of God in a brand new way. May you become a custodian of life changing secrets which God has kept for His sons. Say THAT'S ME!

• **Declaration**

• The favour of the Lord is upon you to transform your world. Those who know you will marvel at what the Lord will do in your life. Fear not the things that seemed to overwhelm you, this is truly your season to manifest. Shout I AM MANIFESTING!

CONCLUSION

Congratulations on taking this special journey to *detox* your spirit and move to a new level in your fellowship with the Holy Spirit. I trust your life has been transformed as you followed this 40 day devotion.

I pray for you to have world taking ideas today. Fresh ideas that will bring you into financial freedom and independence! I pray that toil be broken in your life for good. Say AMEN!

I pray for you for the grace to finish. Whatever you start to do with your hands will prosper. Say I AGREE!

I pray for you for the grace to discern. You will not follow public opinion but the direction God gives. You will not lose opportunities owing to the public sway. Say AMEN!

CPSIA information can be obtained at www.ICGtesting.com
Printed in the USA
LVOW05s2052100314

376789LV00029B/1220/P